WingedPower's Introduction To Psionic Combat

WingedPower's Introduction To Psionic Combat

WingedPower

WingedPower's Introduction To Psionic Combat

By WingedPower

http://www.animaspiritia.com/publications/

ISBN: 978-1-4357-1593-6

Revision: 2

Contents

Introduction

Conflict

Conflict, is inevitable. People eventually have differences of opinion, which cannot be resolved easily through dialogue. When such confrontations occur, the easiest course of action is to resolve one's conflicts, through combat.

Combat and conflict mean different things to different people. To some, it is the means to an end. To others, the combat and conflict is the goal. Perhaps you are currently preparing to battle for a holy cause. Perhaps you are readying to battle for an unholy cause. Perhaps it is for the pride of yourself, or that of your association, be it a clan, a house, a brigade, a guild, or even a loose group of friends. Regardless of the reasons, when you find yourself in a situation where your goal is to fight, then it is of most help, to be able to fight.

Why This Book

Many texts currently available, do not, in my opinion, properly address the issue of combat. More specifically, they do not address the issue of how to employ the energy working skills you are training to improve, for the purpose of doing more than just healing, sensing, or charging. There are precious few books on the subject of employing the craft of the energy worker, towards the goals of the warrior; its use in battle, in war, and its role in combat.

Who This Book Is For

As such, this book is not a beginner's guide to working with energy. It is not a book that will cover, at large, how to go about raising your energy levels through positive attunements. While there is obviously no bias against such skills, as they are useful in the battlefield, there is no point in covering them, as they have been covered quite sufficiently, and to better effect, by other published texts.

You, my dear reader, have chosen to read this book, because its sole focus, is on that of employing energy work, towards the goal of combat.

It is my sincerest hope that you are able to achieve those goals, whatever they may be.

What is Psionics?

In General

Sometimes, it is significantly easier to define what something is not, to better frame the idea, of what it is that one is trying to define.

Psionics is not a game. That is to say, it is not an ability that your character employs through the rolling of dice and counting of points.

Psionics encompasses a body of discussion, skills, and concepts devoted to the study, usage, and research of energy employed by psions. Psionic energy is generated by the body, but which is not of the same quality, density, or usage as life energy, or chi. Such energies are denser than Psionic energy.

Psions manipulate Psionic energy to create a desired effect. This can be to form a shield, perform a scan, create constructs, or to facilitate the exchange of energy. The uses are myriad and limited, only to the psionicists' skill and experience.

In Relation To Combat

In terms of combat, psionics is the means, by which you will generate or gather energy for the intended use of defense, offense, information gathering, and/or communication,

The majority of energy workers and psionicists already know how to employ their craft to form shields, drain energy, blast people with energy, or throw constructs at others. These are very basic skills, which most energy workers are familiar with.

If you are one of those who has learned in a sheltered environment and have found this book, in wonderment, that your craft can be employed to harm others, then please be advised that even without this book, people have been employing energy to harm others. With this book, you have a means by which to increase your ability to defend yourself against such attacks. You do not need to study the offensive ideas and concepts contained within this book, but whether through this text, or others, I implore you. Please, find the time to train properly, so that you can defend yourself against others, who unlike yourself have led less sheltered lives.

Why Learn Such Things?

While you may opt to place this book back on the shelf, that doesn't mean that someone else won't pick it right up, gain the knowledge you chose to pass on, and employ it for purposes that run counter to your philosophies and beliefs.

I do not advocate war and strife. However, I believe that war and strife are often held at bay by the mutual understanding that all parties are participating on equal footing. When that understanding is removed, war and strife inevitably makes an appearance. Why remain at peace, if you can take from those less powerful than you?

Give the other side a run for their money. If you must be a sheep, at least be a sheep with a machine gun.

Summary

- Psionics is a skill you can build up

- Psionic energy comes from within your body and is natural to use

- Energy work can be for offensive as well as defensive purposes

- Others may already be employing similar techniques, defend yourself!

What You Will Need For This Book

Thankfully, you will not need much, in the way of material items, to make full use of this book.

Solo Practice & Exercises

These are exercises, which if you so choose, you can perform on your own. You will require no additional equipment, save yourself, and perhaps a small journal to jot down your experiences and any notes you feel will be useful for later review. It is a great way to measure your progress, as well as your change in perception over time.

Partnered Practice & Exercises

Partnered exercises involve the participation of one other person, with whom you are to work with. These exercises often involve the exchange of energy, testing of shields, or practicing various forms of techniques, where practicing by yourself would be somewhat less productive.

Non attack-based examples of this would be having your partner scan you while you are charging, and noting their results in a separate journal. The addition of another perspective will greatly aid in your development.

The one optional, but highly beneficial, thing you will want is another energy worker or Psion, to practice with. This will make some of the exercises go much easier. It will also help, when it comes to sensing and scanning.

Group Practice & Exercises

Some of the exercises will require at least three members, in order to get adequate effectiveness from the practice session. This includes exercises where you attempt to shield a person, while another person attempts to attack that person. The third person, who is the one being shielded and attacked, is the one who is recording down what effects they sense and the effectiveness of the shielding vs. the effectiveness of the attacks.

Such an exercise, while achievable with only two people, is not nearly as effective as with three.

This will also come into play, later, when you incorporate scavenger hunt-style games.

Core Concepts and Skills

In this book, the primary goal is to get you up to speed on what you need, to be able to effectively spar with another psion, or work in a defensive or offensive manner, as you so chose. To this end, you will need to sharpen and refine your abilities. Specifically, in regards to scanning/remote view, attacks, and defenses.

When I refer to scanning and remove viewing, I am referring to your ability to "see" or "sense" the energy you are working with and the energy that your opponent(s) are working with. In a sense, you are going to be developing your "sight". The more refined your senses are, the more refined your energy work will be, allowing you to be effective at both attack and defense.

The second skill that will be focused on, will be that of defense. Before you begin practicing attacks, you should know how to block. Otherwise, you risk energetic injury to yourself. What's more, there is the off chance that you might draw the attention of uninvited guests or accidentally strike someone you didn't mean to. If they come at you, you should at least be able to shield properly.

Lastly, once you are sensitive enough to see, and good enough at defense, you will focus on using energy in a variety of offensive methods and techniques. Later in the book, I will cover the creation of more complex and useful automated defense and offense systems.

Energy: Where It Comes From

One immutable fact about energy work, of any kind, is that you need energy. This is not a superfluous statement. There are energy workers out there, who will insist that they can do it alone, that all they need is their will, and they can make things happen.

They never care to take a look at whether they have sufficient energy. They never take into account that there are such things as a difference in energy between two people.

Yes, some people are founts of power. But they are not limitless.

To be an effective combatant, you need to know when you are just out of ammo. No matter how skilled you are, if you have nothing left to put into a construct, it won't matter if your construct will be able to power a small city, when it is done. The issue is that it will never get done.

And so, we will talk about energy generation and charging. The exercises listed in the following pages can be performed, either by yourself, or in the company of someone else. The added benefit of having someone else with you, is that the person who is not generating or charging, can practice sensing and viewing, then switch off, taking turns at each task to build proficiency.

A Simple Psionic Energy Charging Exercise

Charging is the act of gathering energy and making it available to you for immediate usage. For example, you would charge your hands, if your intent were to create a psiball, or to perform construct construction.

To charge, it helps to be in a relaxed setting and to be sitting down. When you are more experienced, you will be able to charge at will, without the need for relaxation.

1) While sitting down, rest your hands, palms up, on your knee or armrest of the chair you are sitting in.

2) Visualize your body full of warm water, like a glowing blue substance permeating your whole body. Feel it there, swirling and heavy.

3) Now, focus on the palm of your dominant hand. Focus on the palm of your hand, and visualize the glowing blue warm water flowing and rushing from all over your body, down your arm, and into the palm of your hand.

4) Visualize the glowing blue water pooling and swirling, in the palm of your hand, as more and more water gathers there, it gets heavier and heavier.

This simple exercise allows you to get a feel of what it feels like to charge your hand with energy from other parts of your body. Different people feel the effects to different levels and in different ways. For some, it feels like pooling warm water, cool water, pins and needles, tingling, or an electric sensation. It can be very faint or very strong. It depends on your own body's energy system and how sensitive you are.

If you are the partner who is viewing, you will want to focus on sensing how your partner gathers energy and monitoring the rate of flow and what it looks and feels like to you, without disturbing your partner's exercise. When you trade off, see if you can perform the action faster!

A Simple Psionic Energy Generation Exercise

Now that you've given charging a try, how let's see how generation is similar, but different from charging.

Whereas the act of charging simply brought energy to your hand, the act of generation will attempt to create new energy in your hand. It is, slightly more difficult than charging, but will serve you well, as a developed skill.

As with charging, when you first start out generating, it helps to relax and be seated comfortably

1) While sitting down, rest your hand, palm up on your knees or armrest. Relax.

2) Focus on your hand, and visualize holding a tennis ball in your hand. Feel the fuzzy texture of the ball in your hand. Give it a good squeeze, making its presence there as real as is possible.

3) Now, begin to close your hand on your visualized tennis ball, and just as your hand begins to your mind's command to close on the ball, relax. Do this again a few times, just right before your hand responds to your intent and attempt to close on the visualized tennis ball, relax.

4) Continue this a few times, until you being to feel your hand infused with energy.

Much like charging, generating leaves your hand feeling tingling, warm, cold, or otherwise stimulated. The difference is that instead of just taking Psionic energy from other parts of your body, what you have done is taken physical and electrochemical energy in your physical body to generate Psionic energy in your hand. Congratulations!

This encompasses the basic means, by which to employ the energy that is within yourself, without dependence upon external sources of energy.

However, there are other forms of energy, which can be employed. Being able to control your own energy will allow you better control of other forms of energy. Think of it as a foundation, from which to build upon.

As with the gathering exercise, the partner not performing the active exercise can observe the changes going on as you try to generate. How is your partner generating their energy? Does their process differ from how you generate energy? Who is faster? Who can generate more energy? When you switch off, try to incorporate the technique of your partner and see if it is easier or more difficult.

Observations & Notes

Date / Time :

Using Energy From Other Sources

There are more types of energy than we are aware of. So, please, do not consider the list here exhaustive, as it is most assuredly not.

A Simple Energy Grounding Exercise

Before using other forms of energy, it is worthwhile to learn how to ground yourself. That is, to dump excess energy from yourself, in order to remain balanced and centered.

1) Relax yourself as with the charging and generating exercises.

2) Perform the charging exercise, building up a good charge that you can feel.

3) Visualize a fast growing root system made of energy forming from your feet, going deep into the ground.

4) Visualize and will the energy in your hand flowing into the ground through this massive root system of energy.

5) Visualize the root system pulled back into you.

The grounding exercise is quite simple, and many variations exist. For most, it is as simple as reaching out and grabbing hold of something with their hands, which is in contact with the ground, like a pole, then willing their excess energy into the pole.

Life Energy

The previous section covered basic generation and manipulation of Psionic energy, which is derived from life energy, or core energy. This is the energy that most people think of, when they are referring to one's life force, chi, prana, or perhaps, soul energy.

The quality of life energy is heavier and denser than Psionic energy. It also has more of a "will" to it, and thus it helps to facilitate the creation of autonomous or self-aware constructs.

Unfortunately, unlike Psionic energy, the source of life energy is not well understood, and by extension, the mechanism by which to replenish it, is likewise not well understood.

Eastern energy work, which employs chi, suggests that the increasing of the flow of chi within one's body will help to replenish it, as will the act of breathing and harmonizing with the world.

Those from the Reiki school of thought believe that tapping into a universal power, will allow you to replenish your life energy.

Regardless of the interpretation or philosophy, each person has access to a great deal of life energy. Some believe that they can gain access to even greater stores of life energy, essentially becoming a life energy fountain.

Gathering Life Energy

As with Psionic energy, one can consciously act to concentrate and move life energy within their body. As with Psionic energy, relaxation is key to successful life energy manipulation.

1) Sit down in a comfortable position. Breath deeply and slowly, but otherwise normally. Rest your hands against your pelvis, just under your belly button/navel, at your solar plexus.

2) Close your eyes and empty your mind of thoughts, focusing on a point just below your belly button/navel, slightly above your pelvis. This is your solar plexus.

3) As you notice physical sensations in your body, gently nudge them with your mind towards your point of focus at the solar plexus.

4) Continue this concentration and mental shifting of sensations, all the while, breathing deep, deep into your body.

5) On your in breath, breath deep and down into your solar plexus. On your out breath, let the breath escape slowly, holding the breath in your lungs, pushing down towards your solar plexus.

6) After several cycles of this, you will feel a weight or warmth developing in your solar plexus. While still relaxed, will the weight and warmth to swirl, like a small vortex. Urging it to move faster and faster.

7) There may be an overwhelming urge for this pent up energy to rise up, however, keeping your mind centered and the energy compressed there will allow you to feel the effects of the life energy vs. Psionic energy.

8) When you are ready to end your energy gathering, allow the energy to flow throughout your body, spreading and once again becoming part of you. If you had intent in mind, you would employ the energy for that purpose instead.

Generally speaking, it is very similar to Psionic energy work, and in general, most energy work, on the surface, is quite similar. However, their innate traits differ and the employment of these different energies in your constructs will result in different effects.

The Energy of Other Living Things

Eventually, one will come to the realization that if you can gather energy from within yourself, that you should be able to gather energy from outside of yourself. Yes, that is quite true.

The question then becomes: what kinds of energy can you use, which comes from outside of yourself?

In all honesty, this is where the "more types of energy than one can enumerate" line of thought comes into play. You have faith and/or quantum energy, earth energy, life force from plants and animals, life force from other humans and entities, and various dimensional forms of energy.

For the purpose of this book, we will focus only on the life and Psionic energy of other living beings, to keep the scope of this book narrow. In regards to the Earth, we will treat it as a massive energy sink, to ground energy to. While you can withdraw energy from the Earth, it is something best left for a later addition, on this subject.

Drawing or Vamping Psionic Energy From Another Person

Similar to when you were trying to gather energy from within yourself, you will be best served, by being in a relaxed environment. For this exercise, it may be helpful to have a willing participant, and take turns performing this exercise, switching roles as necessary.

Contact Method

1) Choose one person to be the attacker, and the other to be the victim.

2) Both persons should relax and breathe normally.

3) The attacker should charge their hand, as in the Psionic charging exercise. The Psionic energy formed in the hand should be formed into a flow, like a coiled spring, or tube.

4) The attacker should reach out with their hand and place it on the hand of the victim. When your hands meet, will the Psionic energy in your hand to spring forth, into the hand or arm of the victim, fusing with their energy field.

5) Once you have done this, take in what your body and your senses are telling you. When you feel that you have

established a good bond with the other person, continue onto the next step.

6) Feel the energy flow in both of your bodies, and as with the charging exercise, visualize and will the energy to flow from the victim into your hand, through that energy bond you have formed.

7) Continue this for a little while, and let the energy you have pulled from the other person, flow back into them, so that they can reintegrate it within themselves.

8) Write down your feelings, impressions, and switch places.

The contact method tends to be easier, because physical contact allows one to form a stronger bond with the other individual. This, in turn, allows you to have a higher chance of success.

An alternate, and more common form of this kind of energy interaction occurs without the need for physical contact.

Remote Method

1) Choose one person to be the attacker, and the other to be the victim.

2) Both persons should relax and breathe normally.

3) The attacker should charge their hand, as in the Psionic charging exercise. The Psionic energy formed in the hand should be formed into a flow, like a coiled spring, or tube.

4) Instead of reaching out with one's hand, visualize and will the coiled Psionic flow to flow out and make contact with the victim's energy field, slowly bleeding into the field to form a bond.

5) Once you have done this, take in what your body and your senses are telling you. When you feel that you have

established a good bond with the other person, continue onto the next step.

6) Feel the energy flow in both of your bodies, and as with the charging exercise, visualize and will the energy to flow from the victim into your hand, through that energy bond you have formed.

7) Continue this for a little while, and let the energy you have pulled from the other person, flow back into them, so that they can reintegrate it within themselves.

8) Write down your feelings, impressions, and switch places.

As you can see, the only material difference is whether the person was touched or not. Once you get the hang of the contact method, practice the remote method, until you can do it reliably.

Once you both have been able to successfully pull energy out of one another, try the exercises where the victim isn't passive, but actively works to pull their energy tight within themselves. See who can make it the most difficult for the other person to pull energy from them.

Summary

- Energy can be exchanged between people
- Energy can come from outside of yourself
- Energy can be sent outside of yourself
- Energy can be taken from someone against their will
- The theft of energy can be resisted or stopped

Observations & Notes

Date / Time :

Basic Defense / Shields

While being able to manipulate energy and draw energy from others is useful, you will require more targeted means of defense, in order to be effective, when under even low levels of attack.

Defense takes various forms: barriers, shields, grounding effects, reflection, and absorption/conversion.

Barriers

Barriers are the most simple and basic of shielding principles. You are basically forming a large field of energy around you, where any kinds of attacks need to work their way through this mass, in order to get to you.

Let's try forming a barrier:

1) Relax in a normal setting, breathing normally.

2) Begin to charge up your hands, building up energy by generation.

3) Once your hands are charged, expand that charged field over the whole of your body, eventually covering yourself in Psionic energy.

4) Once you are fully covered, continue to generate energy and reinforce the charged energy around you, expanding it slightly beyond your physical body.

5) Imagine and project the intent of a padded body suit into the energy field around you, knowing that it will slow down any energy sent your way, until it is rendered harmless.

This will create a fairly basic energy barrier around your person, which will act as a cushion against any attacks sent your way.

Note, it will not be able to fend of vamping attacks, any kind of parasite, or advanced forms of penetrating attacks.

Like any barrier, it can eventually be worn down or breached.

Shields

Shields, like barriers, are energy fields that surround you. However, unlike a normal barrier, a shield's aim is to actively repel attacks directed against you. Instead of something soft and fluffy, like dough, you are projecting something more akin to hardened steel.

1) Relax and charge up, as you did with creating a barrier.

2) Form the barrier energy field around your person. Expand it slightly more away from you, letting it take on the form of a sphere around you.

3) Visualize and will your energy barrier to condense, forming a hollow sphere around you, forcing the energy to harden and become more and more dense with each breath.

4) Concentrate on the feel and strength of hardened steel, or the feel of a solid immobile stonewall. Focus on the intent of protection from outside forces, just as a sphere of stone or steel around you would protect you.

The shield created in this form, is essentially a functional construct, whose purpose is to keep things away from you. The shield will be able to better resist attacks directed at you, as well as keep parasites off of your own energy field, as the shield would be a separate object.

Grounding Shields

Sometimes, the form of attack directed at you will be one where you are being charged up with energy. This is called an overload attack. The goal of such an attack is to disrupt your ability to think clearly or manipulate energy properly.

To defend against such an attack, you will need to form a grounding shield. Note, a grounding shield would also work against a vamping attack, where energy is being taken away from you.

1) Relax and begin charging as before, with the barrier and shield.

2) As you begin to feel your body being charged, start forming the dense shield, close to your body. Make it dense and resilient.

3) Extend the bottom of the dense shield, deep into the ground below you, forming strong root systems.

4) Slowly, expand the dense shield, still part of the root system, like a tree stump with a single blossoming flower, with you in the heart of it.

5) Visualize the whole surface of the shield absorbing and transferring energy deep into the Earth, taking energy thrown at it and sending it away, deep into the ground.

Assuming you are under an overload or a vamping attack, it is advantageous to form the shield as close to yourself as possible, as that will allow you to maintain the most control over energy. By expanding the shield, you are essentially brushing and pushing aside any errant energy effects from near you, to a distance further from your energetic self.

Your shield and the root system, essentially becomes an enclosed grounding rod, with you on the inside. Grounding shields are also useful for empaths or those who are sensitive to the energies of large crowds. Form the shield and it will help you deal with malls, concerts, etc.

Reflection Shields

Sometimes, the attack being directed at you is annoying and energetic/patterned in nature. That is, it is packaged with intent and programming. For such attacks, presuming they are not intelligent or programmed to work around reflection can be bounced back at the originator of the attack.

Reflection shields, like grounding shields, are effective for dealing with massive amounts of mental and emotional noise, though unlike the grounding shield, it only sends it back to the sender, as opposed to grounding the noise and energy.

Like the grounding shield, the mirror shield is best formed close to your energetic self.

1) Relax and charge up.

2) Once you have built up some energy and charged up your body, form a dense shield, completely covering your energetic body.

3) Focus on the shield being dense and strong, like steel, as with the normal and grounding shields. Make it dense.

4) Visualize that the outside of the shield, slowly at first, is being polished and made smooth, then gleaming. Until finally, it is reflective like a sphere of mercury, reflecting everything coming into contact with it.

5) Focus your intent into your shield to reflect all attacks and energy directed at it, back at the originator. Command it to remain in place until you release it.

As you might have surmised, the quality and effectiveness of your shield is highly dependent upon your mental focus and clarity. The more focused you are, and the more intent and clear your visualization and intent, the more potent and effective the shielding and constructs will be.

Absorption, Conversion, or Vamping Shields

Yet another kind of shielding is the vamping shield. This kind of shield does not ground, resist, or reflect the energy and attack directed at it. Instead, it takes the patterned energy and de-patterns it, converting it into energy that it can use to power itself. In essence, it feeds on the attacks directed at it. Such shields are often tied to some form of attack mechanism, so that the converted and absorbed energy can be used to power a retaliatory attack.

To create this kind of shield, it would be helpful to do some research into various topics of interest, for inspiration and an understanding of how the concepts work.

- Blenders, grinders/sanders, garbage disposal units, etc.
- Solar furnaces, solar power generation, solar panels, sterling engines
- Corrosive compounds, like sodium hydroxide, strong acids, etc.

Once you have the various concepts in mind, with examples, you may proceed to the creation of your very own vamping shield.

1) As before, relax and being to charge up.
2) When you have the whole of your body charged, form a dense shield around yourself, and expand it to form a sphere.
3) Begin charging yourself again, and form yet another shielding sphere, expanding it to just within the first shield.
4) Focus on the outermost shield and bring to mind the blenders, grinders, disposal units, and rock crushers. Envision the shield being completely covered in incredibly dense and strong crushing teeth, all over the

surface of the outside of the sphere. Anything coming into contact with the outer surface of the sphere will be broken down into fine energetic particles.

5) Now, focus on the inner shield. Picture this shield like the inside of a stomach, flipped inside out, covered in a gel-like digestive compound, riddled with energy sensitive ridges and surfaces, absorbing particulate and energy alike, as it passes through the outer layer of your shield.

6) Focus on these two layers working in harmony with one another, breaking down, filtering, consuming and absorbing the energy and essence of things being directed at you, basking you in the clean and refreshing energy that results.

7) Let your focus of these two layers to become more and more compressed, until they form a single dense hybrid shield. Memorize the resulting pattern, so that you can generate the shield at will, at a later time.

You have the option of employing the energy to launch different attacks, to replenish your own energy field, build additional layers to your shield, etc.

When it comes to shielding, the skies are the limit. You are perfectly free to combine different shields together, to form progressively more and more complex shields, capable of doing more than just merely protecting you.

A popular technique is the inverted shield. Picture an inverted mirror shield formed around someone attacking you with energy blasts.

The limit is your imagination and your mental focus.

Summary

- Shields are only limited by your ability to conceive of what the shield can do

- Shields can reflect attacks

- Shields can absorb attacks

- Shields can ground energy

- Shields can be multi-purpose

- Shields, with practice, can be brought up very quickly

Observations & Notes

Date / Time :

Basic Offense

A great way of testing one's shields is to launch attacks against it. Energy based attacks can take many forms. In fact, the manner in which you can conduct an attack against someone is, in fact, limited only by your imagination and mental endurance.

When it comes to attacking, the most popular, and by far the simplest, is simply to lob a blob of energy at someone or hit him or her with a dart or blast of energy. While easy to perform, they tend to be less effective; as such attacks tend to have little intent behind them.

Having said that, let's look at a couple of exercises.

Lobbing PsiBalls At People

1) Relax and charge up your hand as normal.

2) Focus intently on the palm of your hand and visualize your energy getting denser and denser, building up in the palm of your hand.

3) Place your hands so that they are about 5" apart from one another and focus on energy building up between them, expanding between your hands.

4) Eventually, you will begin to feel a "push" from between your palms, like something soft, like cotton candy. Continue to focus on compressing the energy between your hands, and cupping and pressing your hands together, as if to make a snowball.

5) Once your psiball feels about as dense as you can make it, choosing someone to throw it at. Visualize them clearly in your mind, and as you physically throw the psiball, focus your intent on it hitting them and them reacting.

This is something that works well when you practice with someone else as a target. If you get it on the first try, great! Keep making it denser and denser. If you don't seem to be able to make it work, keep focusing on charging and making the energy dense.

Energy Blasting People

1) As with the Psiball, charge your hands, and build up energy.

2) Pick a target you want to hit with the energy blast.

3) Place your two hands close together, cupping them outward towards the person. Focus on building up energy in your cupped hands. Visualize shaking up a bottle full of soda, and the pressure is building between your hands.

4) When you have as much energy and pressure as you can muster, picture your popping the cork off of the bottle, and the blast of energy striking out at the person you targeted.

As with other practices and exercises, success is a matter of focus, intent, energy buildup, control, and release. Keep practicing. If it helps, for those who are interested in lasers… or just need another analogy for the idea behind emitting a blast of energy:

- Q-switched laser cavities

- Air powered rockets, with the pumping

- Sling and pebble, building up momentum

Those who are more science fiction minded can visualize that they have a energy conversion crystal in their hands and focus their energy into it, to cause it to emit a coherent beam of energy.

Vamping Attacks

1) Choose a target for the attack

2) Charge up and send a link of energy to the person, anchoring deep into the energy field of your target.

3) Once anchored, begin pulling energy from them at a faster and faster rate, either using it yourself or sending it to ground.

Overloading Attacks

1) Choose a target for the attack

2) Charge up and begin to form a link

3) As you send the link out to anchor within the target's energy field, begin massively charging up your field.

4) Once the link is established, send large pulses of energy down the link to your target

Overloading attacks can also be combined with patterns and intents to inflict headaches, pain, or disorientation.

Phased Attacks

A phased attack is one where you are syncing up your attack's frequency or wavelength to one which the shield will allow through, or where the shield is susceptible to damage from. Determining the weak point of a shield or a person's energy field requires diligent practice and training in ones' scanning abilities.

Summary

- Like shields, attacks are only limited by your ability to conceive of the attack
- Certain attacks are only effective against certain types of defenses
- Attacks can be carried out through sending or taking of energy

Basic Scanning

Being able to form shields and basic energy blasts is nice and all, however, not being able to determine what level of effectiveness you are having, renders you essentially blind on the battlefield.

Scanning is one of those soft skills, because it is more about stopping to listen and feel, as opposed to straining to build up energy.

To many, scanning is the less glamorous aspect of energy work, but eventually, everyone realizes that they actually need this skill. Might as well work on it before you become too ingrained in your ways.

To that effect, there are numerous ways to practice energy sensing and scanning techniques. To be effective, however, you should ideally be practicing with at least one other person, so that you can compare what one is projecting and what one perceives.

Partnered Practice and Exercises

Scanning exercises work best with partners. Here are some progressively harder tests that you and your partner can try.

Left Hand, Right Hand

This game is about sensing, which hand is holding the psiball.

One person is the guesser and the other person is the holder.

The holder charges and builds a small dense psiball in one hand, then holds out their hand. The guesser scans the hand to determine which hand is holding the ball.

There should be at least a foot between the holder and the guesser's hands, to avoid picking up on heat/etc.

The holder should mark down which hand, and the guesser should mark down their guess, and compare afterwards.

Guess The Shape

Like the "Left Hand, Right Hand" game, you have someone forming the energy construct, and someone scanning and guessing.

Instead of just a ball, the holder will form one of several pre-determined shapes: a cube, a sphere, a disc/oval, a star (flat), or an X/cross. This item is then held in one hand or the other, after the desired item and hand is noted down by the holder.

The guesser then attempts to scan both hands and make a shape and hand determination.

The results should be compared after a full run has been completed.

Hard or Soft

Like the "Left Hand, Right Hand" game, an energy ball is formed. However, instead of shape, the density of the ball or the hardness of the ball is augmented. This requires better energy control on the part of the holder as well as energy sensitivity on the part of the guesser.

What Changed?

The holder creates an object of certain predetermined features. The holder jots down the characteristics. The holder then gives the object to the guesser. The guesser will note down what they think the object is. Take the energy object, change something about it, jot down their change, and pass it back. The original holder then needs to identify what has changed with the object, and note it down.

Compare notes after exercise. Needless to say, if you can't do previous exercises reliably, then the later exercises will be significantly harder.

What Kind of Shield?

Your partner creates a shield. Once they have created the shield around themselves, they jot down what form of shield they created.

You then scan the shield and determine which kind of shield it is, noting down your scan results. You both compare results and then switch places.

Solo Practice and Exercises

The following exercises can be practiced by one person, or by multiple people.

Shape Retention

In this exercise, what you do is create a dense psiball. Once you have a fairly dense psiball, place it on a table or shelf somewhere, and go away and do something else for a few minutes.

When you come back to the psiball, is it still where you left it? Did it retain its shape? Does it seem different? Note down your observations.

Variations include reinforcing the ball and putting indentation on it and seeing if they remain. Increase the length of time you leave it alone.

Stash Away

Like a game of hide and go seek. Once you have established, from the "Shape Retention" exercise, that you can create a psiball that retains its shape and existence for more than a day, start planting psiballs around your home and workplace.

As you go through your day, scan the room and see if you can sense the presence of these balls. Jot down your experience.

Orientation

Create a psiball and have it form around a coin, or dice. You can either test this with your eyes closed, or employ an opaque cup or mug to perform the flipping/rolling.

Try to sense the orientation of the coin or dice, and note down your impressions. Record down the actual orientation of the coin or dice. Scan the coin or dice while looking at it. What's different?

Summary

- Sensing can be performed on yourself, your constructs, or someone else and/or their constructs
- Sensing allows you to "see" what you are working with
- Sensing can be used to detect things around you, which you cannot see with your physical eyes
- Sensing is crucial for remote attack and defense work

Observations & Notes

Date / Time :

Defending Against Specific Attacks

At this point, you should be adept at the following skills:

- Energy generation/charging and manipulation.
- Creation of the various forms of shields.
- Creation of the basic forms of attacks.
- Be able to make an accurate determination of energy qualities, shapes, and shield types.

For the following exercises, you will want a partner to be with you, one is the attacker, and the other is the defender. If you have a third partner, they can serve as the observer.

For each form of attack, there is a definitive form of defense. However, during the course of a battle, people can change their strategies and techniques, rendering a previously effective defense worthless.

Energy Blasts

The most common type of attack would be the energy blast. Most of the time, this is not intentional and is merely the energy discharge from people having a bad day, disliking you, or perhaps it was intentional. Regardless of the reason, you will need to shield against it and you have a variety of options:

- simple dense energy shield to resist the attack
- reflective energy shield to bounce the attack back
- absorption energy shield to make use of the energy
- grounding energy shield to send the energy into the Earth

Each of these defense methods can be tried out by you and your partner(s) with one person forming one of the shields listed above and the attacker, sending progressively stronger psi blasts at the shield. The observer and attacker should both take note of how effective the blasts are.

Overloading Attacks

An overload attack is a means of disabling your target by filling them with too much energy, thus overloading their energy system. This may disorient them, get them confused, upset them, or they might not even feel it, if they can handle large amounts of energy or are a psi-vamp.

Defenses against such an attack includes:

- grounding shield
- absorption shield
- reflection shield
- shielding the attacker and cutting them off from their energy source

When it comes to overloading attacks, your first priority is to dump the excess energy out of your system, so that you can regain control. One good way to do this is to ground, or to form a massive shield. The best way to stop the attack is to cut the attacker off from their energy source, if they are employing an extenal source, or to just route them to ground via a shield. Some, who have larger energy capacities, may opt to increase the flow of energy and just vamp the attacker and send that energy to ground, exhausting the attacker.

Vamping Attacks

Like the overloading attack, but in the opposite direction. This kind of attack seeks to deprive you of energy. The defense against this is similar to the overloading attack, but with opposite intentions!

You can defend against this attack by:

- forming a shield around the attacker to prevent them from grounding the energy properly, effectively turning their vamp attack into a self-overloading attack

- create a grounding shield

- vamp the attacker back!

Depending on the reason why a vamping attack is being employed, the above techniques may have various levels of effectiveness. The best bet would be to first shield yourself, to reduce and offload the strain of having energy being taken from you. The second, is to determine if this is a psi-vamp or a normal psion who is using a vamping technique. If the attacker is not a psi-vamp, then shield them from ground and they will get overloaded. If they are a psi-vamp, then tether or link your shield's energy source to something negative, like ground, and the psi-vamp should, eventually, disengage.

Sensation Projection / Offensive Shielding

If your opponent is using an inverted shield or other construct system that is surrounding you to attack you, then please refer to the next section, detailing how one is to get past shields, as that is what you are dealing with.

Summary

- Attacks are based on the flow of energy
- Overloading attacks need energy from somewhere and that energy needs to go somewhere
- Vamping attacks pull energy from somewhere and depending on the attacker, is either consumed or grounded
- Most attacks have a suitable defense, save massively brute force techniques

Observations & Notes

Date / Time :

Getting Past Shields

At this point, you should be adept at the following skills:

- Energy generation/charging and manipulation.
- Creation of the various forms of shields.
- Creation of the basic forms of attacks.
- Be able to make an accurate determination of energy qualities, shapes, and shield types.

Once you have reached this point, you will be able to start tackling the exercises involved in how to penetrate a particular kind of shielding. The reason why the above skills need to be available is that penetrating a shield requires you to be able to see the shield, to understand the workings of the shield type detected, and have control of energy to work your way past the shield in question.

Lacking in any one doesn't mean you can't get past a shield, only that you will be less effective at it than someone who is adept at the required skills.

Getting Past Barriers

Barriers are the simplest of shields and can be overcome in a variety of ways:

- Vamping attacks
- Vamping shields (inverted)
- Grounding attack (vamp into ground)
- Brute force (blast attack that just forces its way through the barrier)

The technique, which will have the least amount of success, is the brute force method, unless you seriously outclass your opponent, in terms of raw energy.

Since barriers are just dense fields of energy, vamping attacks work best. Grounding attacks can serve as a passive attack vector, while you employ active vamping.

An overload would not work well, as the energy would just be dissipated into the barrier itself.

Getting Past Basic Shields

Shields, which focus on being a hard/solid/strong barrier to entry, can be defeated in a variety of ways:

- Vamping can weaken the shield, reducing it to the status of a barrier.

- Brute force can work to weaken the shield's structure.

The issue with basic dense shields is that they are dense. Your goal is to lower that density via vamping, or weaken the intent or structure of the shield, via brute force.

Other methods you can use to bypass such shields involves stunning or phasing.

Stunning is like a flash grenade. That is, it doesn't do actual physical harm, but it disorients you. So, in the case of a dense energy shield, while one is thinking "strong like steel", in reality, what is being made is more like "strong like bulletproof glass". If you create an intense psionically "bright" flash broadcast, this will disrupt the focus of the opponent, allowing you to breach their shields.

Phasing is a technique that exploits the holes that naturally occur in shields and frequencies. Most people understand phasing to mean "going out of phase", in relation to energy and matter around them. The energy attack equivalent is to scan the shield and determine which frequencies that shield is occupying, and which frequencies it isn't covering. Once you have located those "windows", you will be able to switch to those frequencies, and getting your attacks in, through the shield.

Getting Past Grounding Shields

The key to a grounding shield working is its access to ground, or Earth. The best way to do this is to place a reflective shield or a vamping shield around someone's grounding shield.

Without somewhere for the energy to go, the grounding shield basically operates like a vamping shield, except without a way for the shield to dump energy. So, once you have negated the grounding feature of a grounding shield, energy directed at the shield gets converted into an overload attack.

An alternative to shielding the grounding shield from ground is to super saturate the region that that shield is grounding to. When the natural ground is charged higher than you, the energy flow will reverse, similarly causing an overload attack, which seems to come from nowhere.

Getting Past Reflective Shields

Reflective shields are essentially basic shields, but with programming to reflect attacks back at the original source. One can use this to their advantage, by forming an inverted mirror shield, powered by an external source, then launching attacks into the space between the two shields. Any attack originated from within the shield would be reflected back by your shield onto their shield.

One can also employ the phased shield penetration technique, as there is no such thing as a perfect mirror.

One can also simply vamp a reflective shield, as vamping draws energy away from something, so, depending on the programming of the shield, may not constitute an attack.

Getting Past Absorption, Conversion, or Vamping Shields

It should be noted that an inverted absorption shield would be a good counter to all of the above shield types. Just be sure to create multiple waves of such an inverted shield attack, to ensure that as the shield in front breaks apart and fails, the one behind it is there to keep up the attack.

Ironically, that means that an inverted absorption shield is the best bet to take down an absorption shield around your target.

Failing that, your next best bet is to employ phasing or brute force.

Summary

- There is no such thing as a "perfect shield"

- All shields have a weakness that your opponent will eventually find!

- All shields have a weakness that you will eventually be able to use!

- The greater your arsenal of attacks and energy manipulation ability, the better your ability to penetrate a shield

- Accurate remote viewing is crucial to knowing if you've actually pierced a shield!

Observations & Notes

Date / Time :

Construct Project #1 : Replicating Javelin Launcher Defense Shield

So far, all of the techniques discussed or illustrated have required your immediate attention and participation. In order to wage war, you apparently need to be present.

However, building shields and psiballs falls into a skill category referred to as building constructs.

A construct, or thought form, is basically energy given form and intent. Most constructs are not intelligent, but some imbue them with some of their own life force, in addition to the normal Psionic energy, giving them various degrees of automation and independence.

A note of warning: Constructs have been known to go wild and have needed to be put down or destroyed. Employing life energy or other animated forms of energy into the construction of your construct, or the omission of a "kill switch" or "self destruct switch" in a construct is hazardous.

Having said that, let's discuss several constructs, which when put together, will form the base for a defensive platform.

Javelin Darts

If you have built psiballs and performed psiblasts, you might have noticed that durability isn't really very good. One way to get around this is to increase the density of the energy of the construct.

In this case, what we will be doing is create a construct, which serves as a good penetration missile.

1) Charge up, and gather energy into a mass between your hands.

2) Compress and condense the energy, as if you were going to make a really dense psiball.

3) As the psiball starts forming up, focus intently on the shape of a long stiff javelin, made of diamond hard steel.

4) Keep focusing and picturing, as you pour energy into the construct you are forming. Feel the incredibly needle sharp points on both ends. Feel the heft and density of the javelin dart.

5) Now, form a second cloud of energy around the javelin dart and condense it into a thin, dense shield, molding itself to the shape and form of the construct, to give the form more structure. Like a jacketed bullet, your javelin is now formed.

6) Take note of the pattern and signature of your new high-density missile.

You will want to test this new construct, by finding a target that is shielded. In all likelihood, if you launch it at your target with sufficient energy, it will pierce or embed itself, partially penetrating a shield, quite effectively.

However, it is difficult for you to continually produce these javelins to launch and maintain an offensive.

Hence…

Javelin Replication Construct

The goal of this construct is to rapidly produce high-density javelin darts for attacking a particular target. The replication construct serves as manufacturing construct, as well as missile launcher. The only downside is that it requires an immense amount of power to keep it going.

1) Being to charge up and amass a large cloud of energy.

2) Continue to bring the cloud down until it is just slightly larger than your javelin dart. You still have the original dart and pattern/signature, right?

3) Shape the construct into a rough tube, and as you condense the form down into a heavy and firm form, focus your intent on its ability to convert energy and thoughts about a target, to create the javelin dart rapidly, programming them each to go after the target you had in mind.

4) Continue to focus your intent as you pour energy into the device, until you feel the device basically, "click" having been made solidly and completely enough to achieve the task.

5) Take note of the construct's signature and pattern, keeping not of it for later reference.

6) Hold the construct in your hands, the business end facing away from you. Focus your intent on a target, which is shielded and send energy into the device. Feel the hum of the device as it launches massive numbers of high-density darts at the target.

If the operation of the construct is slow or doesn't seem to work right, dispel it and try again, being sure to keep your intent and focus razor sharp. The better you make the construct, the better it will perform.

However, now that you have an easy to use offensive construct, how do you make it automatic… better question, how do you power the sucker?

Absorption Shield + Replication Array

The answer, of course, is to create a standard absorption shield around yourself, which dumps the energy it produces, into an array of these replication/launcher devices.

1) Charge up and form a absorption shield as described in earlier parts of the book.

2) Once your absorption shield is complete and merged into one dense hybrid layer, create and embed multiple replication launchers at various points in your shield.

3) Focus your intent on linking the energy flow from the shield to the construct launchers, with the shield deriving the originator of the attacks, and sending that information to the replication launchers, along with the energy from the absorbed attacks.

Try out your new auto-defense shield system by having a well-shielded friend launch an energy attack at your shield and have someone else scan the resulting action.

Viral Javelin Darts

What is better than a high-density penetration dart? A highly infectious, replicating missile. For this to work, however, you will need to incorporate a little life energy into the darts, when you first make them, and likewise do the same for the replication launcher.

When creating the darts, and focusing on the intent of being dense and penetrating, also focus on the intent to absorb energy from its target, upon penetration/contact, and use that energy to replicate itself, embedding those copies into the target as well, spreading like a viral rash, and drilling into the energy medium of the target.

When focusing your intent on the viral aspect, visualize and feel a small stream of your core life energy being woven into the structure of the javelin dart, giving it, essentially, life.

Once this is completed and your javelin dart is shielded, you will need to rebuild the replication launcher in a similar way, with the same introduction of a little life energy into the replication launcher with the intelligence to create viral replicating javelin darts.

The absorption shield does not need to be rebuilt, but you can program it to absorb and consume life energy from insects and such, to add life energy to the constructs, to make them more viral and adept at replication.

Javelin Dart Swarms

The javelin darts can also be used, en masse, as a form of both defense and offense. Picture, if you will, a large number of these, swarming and streaming together, like large clouds of insects. These can be used to effect shielding, by surrounding targets in need of defense, or to perform brute force attacks, by forming the head and body of a barrage.

They can also be used to create massive shape shifting shields for other constructs, which may be more delicate in nature.

Observations & Notes

Date / Time :

Construct Project #2: Regenerating Shield

Shields get worn down, holes get poked, structure and programming weakens or become corrupted. Wouldn't it be nice if you had some automated way of repairing, regenerating, or outright replacing shields depleted beyond repair.

The question is whether you want to repair, replace, or augment your shields mid-battle?

Continual Shield Reinforcement

To continually reinforce your shields, you can create a construct, or swarm of constructs, which roams the inner surface of your shields and continually adds to it, thus ensuring that your shield is of a particular thickness, condition, or level of repair.

To form the construct(s):

1) Charge up your hands and form a basic psiball.

2) Once formed, increase the density of the psiball, until it is as solid as you can make it.

3) Focus your intent into the psiball, that it will roam the inner surface of your shields, and continually repair any weaknesses and/or holes in your shield, filling it back in, and reinforcing the programming of the shield.

4) Continue to focus this intent into your psiball, until you feel that the psiball is as focused as you can make it.

5) Take note of this psiball's signature and energy pattern.

6) Place the psiball on the inner surface of your shield, and will it to begin.

7) Repeat for as many shield repair and reinforcement psiballs as you need.

Continual Shield Layering & Replacement

This technique bears more similarities to that of how your skin works. For example, your skin is made up of layers. Your shield can likewise be built up from layers.

When you form your shield, take note of the kind of shield that it is.

1) Charge up your hands and form a basic psiball.

2) As you begin to make the psiball denser, focus your intent and will on the psiball to pulse and emanate and expanding field, that is similar to your shield.

3) As this pulse expands, like the formation of your shield, it will become denser and become filled with intent, expanding and becoming more real and focused.

4) Each of these pulsed expanding shields will eventually reach the size of your current shield, pressing up on it from the inside, forming a new layer.

5) Place this new psiball in your energy field and let it continually form and expand shields, building up layer upon layer.

Alternately, you can program the psiball to automatically form random types of shields as well as shields that are different kinds of frequencies, to make the task of penetrating your shields that much harder.

Observations & Notes

Date / Time :

Construct Project #3: Replicating Vampric Blob Swarm Construct

Ever wish you could drop a paint bucket onto your opponents' proverbial "windshield"? What if you could place just a few droplets, and have it balloon into a full-blown can of paint?

To do this, we will, as in the case of the javelin dart, create a missile, then create the replication launcher.

Creating The Vampric Blobs

1) Charge your hands as before, forming a psiball.

2) Focus your intent, as you condense the ball, of sticky goo, like balls of sticky mud. Focus the intent of psionic forms of leeches swirling and multiplying in the psionic ball of mud.

3) As the ball becomes larger and denser, form a shield around the ball, to keep it stable enough to be launched, but weak enough to break on contact with another's shield, spreading the goo and the vampric leeches.

4) Once you have this ball formed as densely as you can, take note of the signature and the pattern.

Creating The Blob Replicator

The easiest way to create a replication construct for the blobs is to start off with a replicator that you have already created, and modify it, or expand on its abilities. So, assuming you had created the javelin replicator construct, you can now employ it in the creation of a vampric blob replicator.

1) Bring into being, the javelin replicator.

2) Reach in and remove the javelin archetype from the replicator and place the blob psiball archetype into the replicator.

Focus the intent on the replicator to accept and replicate the new archetype. Now, mount it wherever you wish and power it from an appropriate source, and you will be able to shower a target with sticky vampric psiballs.

Observations & Notes

Date / Time :

Construct Project #4: Building Your Own Golem/Guardian/Sentry

So, while all of those automated defense systems are great and fine, what if you prefer the company of humanoid shaped guardians and sentries?

This is, of course, fairly straightforward to do, though perhaps more difficult than most anything else that has been covered so far. Some people may find this easier than other exercises, so your mileage and experience may vary!

The basic idea and premise behind a guardian is that it is sentient, to a degree, and can do things on your behalf:

- creation of constructs
- perform defense functions
- perform offense functions
- gather intelligence and facilitate remote viewing

At this point, you have the option of either imbuing the guardian with some life force, to give it more resilience, or not. It really is up to you. For your first several, you may opt to not. I would also like to stress that you should install a kill switch into your guardian, during its programming.

While you are creating the following basic guardian, consider what it is that you would like your final guardian to do.

Creating The Form of the Guardian

Guardians typically have a form. Most people choose human forms for guardians, because they would like a human companion. Others, choose animal forms, like wolves, dogs, snakes, falcons, dragons, etc. For the purpose of this exercise, we will choose the form of a small child.

1) Picture, in your mind, a small humanoid child form and shape, devoid of details, gender, or ethnicity. Do this while you are generating energy and forming it between your hands.

2) When you have the form of the child in your mind, shape the energy in front of you, until it is in the shape of a small child, but still devoid of details or even a face.

3) Continue to reinforce and make the form denser. Focus your intention and will on the form being your servant. The servant obeys you. Does your bidding. Obeys your will.

4) Once you have the form solidified as much as you can, will it to retain its form and to do your bidding.

At this point, you have created a mindless golem. It is a blank template for you to build future customized golems and guardians from. Its only mind is that of obeying what you tell it to do.

Programming And Ordering Your Guardian

Now that you have a form for your guardian, it is time to imbue it with function. So, let's say you want it to perform guard duty for you, automatically protecting you from harm, and scaring away people and things that might want to negatively influence you.

You may also, at this point in time, want to have some easy way to focus on your guardian, without having to summon it up. A communications device for your guardian, for instance.

In this case, we will use a private notepad. Pen and paper as an additional and alternative means of communicating with your guardian.

Take a notepad that you use for nothing else and has nothing written in it. If no such thing exists in your home, take some blank sheets of paper and staple them together.

1) Charge up and take the notepad in your hands, filling the sheets with your energy.

2) Form a link from the notepad to the child-form you created, willing that in addition to your direct mental commands, anything you write in this notepad, is likewise a command for the guardian to perform.

3) See the link solidify, bonding the guardian and the notepad together.

Now, your notepad is your physical means of ordering the guardian around, giving it commands, like "watch over the following people and things: me, my sister, my cat, my car, my house, etc."

As time goes on, your guardian, through interactions with you and with others, will begin to form a mind of its own. This can be assisted along, but reaching out to it with your mind, and communicating with it.

Arming and Armoring Your Guardian

Well, a guardian wouldn't be much of a guardian, if it had no means by which to effect defense. You can summon up the various defense constructs and embed/link them to the notepad, giving each a symbol or name, and writing down that the guardian may use those constructs for defense and offense. Similarly, you can state under which conditions, each kind of shielding will be employed and which kinds of retaliation should be employed or not employed.

Employing the notepad for this purpose, makes it easier for you to keep track of what you have and have not told the guardian to do. When you are done with one command, cross out the command, stating in your mind, that by crossing it out, you are commanding your guardian to disregard that particular command.

Care and Feeding

Your guardian needs energy to survive. This is something you can program it to do for itself. To take energy from the trees, the insect life, from the Earth, etc. If you have it take energy from people, some might retaliate and destroy your guardian. It can also instill a will into the guardian that might resist your control, so that is not recommended.

It is also recommended to take note of the signature and pattern of your guardian, and in a non-command notebook, write down how you created the guardian, what steps you took, and what the effect was like.

Communicating With Your Guardian

Each person communicates differently. Personally, I have found that the easiest way to communicate is to mentally talk to your guardian through your link with the guardian. This can be mental voices, mental imagery, or just subconscious access to information. You can also perform remote viewing through your guardian, through the link.

Those who employ pendulums and automatic writing techniques, can link the guardian to your hand and ask questions, and have the guardian guide your hand's response, to get the answer you seek. Slower and more limited in range of responses, but can be helpful for those who don't trust their ability to mentally communicate or fear mental contamination.

Observations & Notes

Date / Time :

References

Knowledge does not spring forth from the vacuum. It comes from the positive, and sometimes negative, interaction between different individuals and groups seeking knowledge.

While quite a few have the combat ideas are my own, much of the foundation of energy work relating to Psionics can be attributed to the following main reference sources.

The references list is not an all-inclusive list, but just the big three. There are countless others in the IRC forums, who have discussed such topics with me, as well as those in other, non-psionics related forums.

To those who came before me, and whom I have had the good fortune of working with, I am deeply thankful. To those who are yet to come, I welcome you with open arms and an open mind.

ANKA's Training Manual

ANKA's training manual is the definitive source for training exercises and routines dedicated to getting the beginning energy worker or Psion, onto a proven regiment and having them work their way up to a skilled user of Psionics in no time.

ANKA also develops various Psionic devices, which amplifies and enhances a psion's natural and developed abilities.

You can find excerpts of ANKA's Training Manual, published with his permission, at the Psion Guild address below. His work is copyrighted, and thus is not reproduced in this book. If/when he publishes a book, I would wholeheartedly recommend it, as his work is as good as gold.

ANKA, thank you for your always taking the time to explain, what must have been blatantly obvious, to me again and again.

Winged Wolf's Energy Work Books

WingedWolf and her Psion Guild have proven to be a priceless wellspring of knowledge and information. It would be enough, if that was all there is to it. WingedWolf is also a person of great patience and good humor. Her willingness to take time out to work on an organization dedicated to a place where others can gather and work towards developing their talents and abilities is truly inspiring.

Her research into the base types of various Psions, the characteristics of individuals who are, by default, imbued with different traits and how those traits can be augmented, forms a body of truly useful knowledge.

It is actually her publication of online texts, which inspired me to work on and publish this book.

- http://www.lulu.com/content/287826

- http://www.lulu.com/wingedwolfpsion

WingedWolf, thank you, you're the one who serves as both inspiration and beacon for me to always return to the Psion Guild forums! Hopefully, I won't disappear too often!

The Psion Guild, Forums, and IRC channel

The Psion Guild has been around for quite a while, and serves as repository of Psionic knowledge, split between the knowledge of the members, and that of the online discussion forums.

http://www.psionguild.org/

The Guild organizes a yearly camping trip, where members can gather and meet one another face to face, and work on their Psionic abilities, close to nature.

My shouts go out to NoMad, WingedWolf, Ancient_Arcana, Daimon, Miri, Fenix, and many more, who participated in my various discussions and who have helped me in my own development along the way. Thank you! If I missed your name, I'm very sorry!

"Uncle Chucky" (Charles W. Cosimano)

Uncle Chucky was and is a pioneer in the field of psionics, in regards to radionics and other enhancement devices. His dark humour and off the wall ideas are a true inspiration to those who seek to explore the various corridors of psionic combat and warfare.

http://www.geocities.com/c_cosimano/

My Thank You

For those of you who took the time to buy this book, I thank you and hope that you use it in good health and for greater understanding of both yourself and the world around you.

Your purchase of this book helps to fund future books.

I encourage you to check out the Psion Guild forums, take advantage of the wisdom and knowledge that is being shared there.

Those with questions, or who are interested in other books I have published, can get in contact with me via:

Email: wingedpower@animaspiritia.com

WWW: http://www.animaspiritia.com/publications/

Lulu: http://www.lulu.com/wingedpower

Thank you, for helping to make my book a success.

WP.

www.ingramcontent.com/pod-product-compliance
Ingram Content Group UK Ltd.
Pitfield, Milton Keynes, MK11 3LW, UK
UKHW031050260726
13965UKWH00006B/1332